MODERN ICONS

LED ZEPPELIN

Acknowledgments

With very grateful thanks to Philip Dodd, Morse Modaberi,
Helen Johnson and to Michael Heatley,
Northdown Publishing and the staff of the National
Sound Archive for their help in the research of this book.

Tony Horkins is *Melody Maker*'s technical editor as well as a
freelance journalist for publications as varied as *Empire, Elle, Sky*
and the *Daily Mail*. He has also been editor of the *Virgin Rock
Yearbook*, and in 1996 was part of Goldbug, whose cover version
of Led Zep's 'Whole Lotta Love' reached the UK Top 3.

Modern Icons conceived and developed
for and with Virgin Publishing Ltd by Flame Tree Publishing,
a part of The Foundry Creative Media Company Limited,
The Long House, Antrobus Road, Chiswick, London W4 5HY.

ISBN 0-312-17938-3

Library of Congress Cataloging-in-Publication Data available on request

First published in the United Kingdom in 1997 by Virgin Publishing Ltd.

First U.S. edition

10 9 8 7 6 5 4 3 2 1

MODERN ICONS

LED ZEPPELIN

Introduction by Tony Horkins

St. Martin's Press
New York

CONTENTS

CONTENTS

INTRODUCTION

So what makes an iconic rock figure? The durability of their material? The amount of units they've shifted? A history of impressive chart placings? Well, possibly, but there's no image quite so simply and clearly indicative of a band's iconic status than their ability to be identified in silhouette. And as recognisable as the London skyline, Robert Plant's mane of curly hair and Jimmy Page's laid-back, double-necked guitar swagger were all you needed to know that you were in the presence of the ultimate rock band: Led Zeppelin.

Formed in the late Sixties from the ashes of wannabe icons The Yardbirds and recognisable players on the burgeoning London session scene, Led Zeppelin were always destined for big things. It took just thirty hours of recording and mixing time to pull together a debut album, but its abandoned approach, bone-crunching guitar and ear-shattering vocals set a new standard for the term Heavy Metal.

However it was Led Zep's bending of heavy metal's stiflingly strict rules and regulations that contributed to their longevity. The initial physical package may have been off-the-peg rock circa late Sixties, but the music suggested both an influence and a level of creativity way beyond what was expected of the genre.

That shouldn't have come as too much of a surprise to their record company, Atlantic, who knew they had something a little special on their hands. Which is why they offered the freshly minted band the most substantial deal of the period, a $200,000 advance – enough to put a bustle in anyone's hedgerow. In the Led Zep camp, however, there was never any doubt that they could attract anything but the best and the biggest the industry and its fans could offer. Led Zeppelin only ever thought big.

Before they were even airborne, they'd been busy making their presence known as individuals. Bass player John Paul Jones was already a prominent figure in the airless world of session playing. He'd been picking up regular pay cheques laying a bass foundation for acts as diverse as Marianne Faithfull, PJ Proby, Burt Bacharach, Etta James, Lulu, Tom Jones, Dusty Springfield and the brothers Walker and Everly, cramming in three sessions a day with time to spare for a TV jingle or two.

When Jones wasn't playing bass, his talents were stretched further as an arranger. The original Radio One theme – that was his. Donovan's 'Hurdy Gurdy

Man' and 'Mellow Yellow' and Jeff Beck's 'Hi-Ho Silver Lining' also found their crotchets and quavers in order thanks to a little help from Jones. All this skill, and that was just from the bass player. Led Zeppelin were going to have to find a pretty extraordinary drummer to keep up with him.

Which, of course, they did in the shape of Birmingham-born John Bonham: big man, big drums, big sound. Only twenty-one years old when he joined the fledgling Led Zep, he was too young to have a lengthy, illustrious career behind him, but he'd made enough of a noise backing the little known Tim Rose to attract the attention of Jimmy Page.

Page was quoted as saying he felt Bonham to be the most inventive drummer he'd ever heard, and live and unleashed in Led Zeppelin he proved that he could easily keep up with his more established and experienced new work chums. But for his culpability in inventing the half-hour drum solo, he couldn't put a foot, pedal or stick wrong.

His enormous drum sound and metronomic skills played a critical part in the success of Led Zeppelin. No fan of the controlled studio sound, Bonham threw gaffer tape to the wind and let his drumheads flap free, whether playing them conventionally or, less predictably, with his bare hands.

While his contemporaries fretted about precise microphone positioning and zero room resonance, Bonham was quite happy to thrash away at the bottom of Headley Grange's stately stairway with a single mike hanging off the balcony. The result? A unique sound that guaranteed both him and his band a place in rock's history as innovators.

Led Zeppelin also aquired a reputation as hell raisers. Chucking the TV from the window of your local, friendly Holiday Inn may seem like a rock cliché now, but it took Bonham and co., often with a little help from The Who's Keith Moon, to set the standard. Unfortunately, in more recent times that example has been followed in feeble manner by today's young rockers, who think that dribbling their beer and not making their bed is a strike against the establishment.

Ultimately, however, such excesses took their toll, though it needed more than Bonham's accidental and inevitably drink-related death in September 1980 to silence him, and his sound has lived on. He remains one of the most widely sampled drummers in contemporary music, his inimitable work on 'When The Levee Breaks' continually cropping up as a rhythmic life-saver for dance music producers looking for just a little more swing.

For all their heavy metal histrionics, it was Led Zeppelin's ability to turn a head-banger into a toe-tapper that raised them above the stodgy quagmire of their peers. Not a show band in the traditional sense of the term, it was nevertheless their sheer sense of showmanship that allowed them to stand out from the crowd.

As showy as Bonham's barehanded beating was, it was Jimmy Page's penchant for excessive looking guitars, including his trademark Gibson double-neck, and his occasional desire to trade his plectrum for a violin bow that helped give Led Zep a visual hook in performance.

Along with John Paul Jones, Page had cut his teeth as a session player, backing the likes of The Stones, The Kinks and Donovan, though the great unwashed knew him better as the man who ultimately and confidently replaced both Eric Clapton and Jeff Beck in The Yardbirds.

This was the late Sixties, and soon Page's think-big attitude started pervading the Yardbirds' sound. On their final US tour, they were heard to perform 'I'm Confused', later 'Dazed And Confused', and 'White Summer', which also became part of Zep's repertoire. By the summer of 1968 it was all over for the original Yardbirds, and Page had a decision to make. A ten-day Scandinavian tour with 'The New Yardbirds', or form his own band. Thankfully, the decision came easily. After all, now he was the grand old age of twenty-three.

So he took his low-slung Les Paul and his Marshall stack, turned it up to 11, and re-invented the blues. The world hadn't seen his type or heard his sound before, and suddenly a surfeit of would-be guitar heroes had to find a way to play the guitar as it dangled around their knees.

Not that Page was unable to explore his more sensitive side as a guitar player. But loud rock music and acoustic guitars had never been happy bedfellows, and a surfeit of virtuosity was unheard of in such a basic art form. To begin with this proved all too much for the more simplistic tastes of the American market, and an early US review considered the band to be "loud, impersonal, exhibitionistic, violent

and often insane". What's more, they said it like this might be a *bad* thing . . . .

What the critic hadn't twigged, however, was that Page had a masterplan, and knew exactly how he was shaking up music's aristocracy. And he realised that the success of his mission relied

heavily on the recruitment of the lead vocalist of another Birmingham-based outfit, the less-than-legendary Hobbstweedle. Step forward, Mr Robert Plant.

In fact, Plant didn't just step, he strutted, swaggered and preened while he was at it too. No sooner had he taken to the stage as Led Zep's front man, than he re-defined absolutely what a rock star should look like and sound like. When a spotty, greasy-haired teenager stood in front of the mirror, his fantasy-fuelled mind could metamorphose his hair brush into a microphone and his body into Robert Plant's.

The twenty-one-old singer's lungs had all the power of Bonzo's drum kit, and the bad news was that at one of his first Zep gigs his screaming vocals left the speaker system in tatters. However, the good news was that it just didn't matter. The audience could hear him at the back of the auditorium over the whole group anyway.

And if they couldn't hear, they could gawp. Snakeskin boots, progeny-threatening tight bell-bottomed jeans, flowing open shirt and *that* hair. For the first time, the words 'rock' and 'God' could legitimately be used in the same sentence. And they frequently were.

Keith Moon, or John Entwistle, or possibly both, joked that the combined ensemble would go down like a 'lead Zeppelin', and suddenly a moniker for the approaching mayhem was duly recorded and registered. Now all they had to do was make a record.

After their initial reticence, the Americans lapped up 'Led Zep I's largely blues-fuelled workouts, the Brits jumping on board their star-bound balloon for 'Led Zep II' and its now-legendary inclusion,

'Whole Lotta Love', a million-selling hit single in the US, but never released in Britain. In fact, Zep weren't big on releasing singles, but singalong gems were to be found amongst the lengthy workouts and more than occasional self-indulgences that dominated a lot of their output.

'Led Zep III' gave us 'Immigrant Song'; the

fourth (untitled) album 'Black Dog', 'Rock And Roll' and every music-shop owner's worst nightmare, 'Stairway To Heaven', destined to be massacred whenever an aspiring guitarist asked to test a new guitar. 'Houses Of The Holy' offered 'The Song Remains The Same', 'Physical Graffiti' produced the most expensive album sleeve ever conceived and the truly hypnotic 'Kashmir', 'Houses Of the Holy' and 'Trampled Under Foot'. But although 1976's 'Presence' included 'Achilles Last Stand' and 'Nobody's Fault But Mine', the album – recorded shortly after Plant's near-fatal car crash in Greece – lacked the distinction and direction of previous recordings. Their finest hour had ticked its last and time was moving on.

In late 1976 the band released the soundtrack to one of the most self-indulgent rock movies ever made. 'The Song Remains The

Same', with its bloated workouts of the classics, and the two subsequent albums (including 'Coda', released after Bonham's death), were evidence that Led Zeppelin's glory days had passed.

For the punk movement, Led Zep were an aging anachronism. Upstaged by the new wave, their kind of rock stood as a monument to a time that many wished to forget. Their excesses could only be enjoyed by the privileged, their sound by those not yet tuned in to the tighter, crisper and earthier noise of a new generation. Besides, the new kids on the block couldn't afford the drugs.

And their extravagant tours, the undoubtedly apocryphal stories of hotel orgies involving groupies and various branches of the fish family, the pomp and occasional pomposity, all became the blueprint for an easily parodied image of 'the quintessential rock band'. No one captured that image as tartly or as brilliantly as the 'Spinal Tap' team. When Nigel Tufnell performs his virtuoso guitar solo, using not merely a violin bow on the strings, but producing a

complete violin, the reference was not even thinly disguised.

Although in the later stages, Led Zeppelin, perhaps inevitably, began to lose the focus and direction of their early years, their apparently irresistible rise from 1968 onwards had been masterminded by another iconic figure, the fifth member of the band, manager Peter Grant. Shadowing them like a stalker, Grant was up there with Colonel Tom Parker and Brian Epstein as one of the new breed of celebrity managers, striking, quite literally at times, the fear of the devil into all he crossed, and duly earning his reputation as the fiercest and most feared of rock managers.

Happily encouraging his boys to live life large, he re-drafted the role of the manager by doing exactly the same. He travelled with the band, toured with them and indulged with them. His methods served as a model for all who followed, the opening chapter in the How To Be A Rock Manager handbook.

Grant died in 1995, but his legacy lives on. The influence of the band that he and Page created, and in which every member became a quintessential representative of their particular art, is still to be found in the work of an eclectic mix of newer music makers. Without Zep, would the Eighties have been so kind to rock acts like Def Leppard, AC/DC and Iron Maiden? Would The Cult have sounded quite so raw? Would the Beastie Boys have sounded quite so groovy? Would Frankie have gone to Hollywood, or U2 left Ireland? Would Lenny Kravitz ever have written a song?

Like it or not, the answer's a resounding no . . . .

Tony Horkins

LIVE AND EXPLOSIVE

• •

Although the band's guitarist and producer Jimmy Page lavished hours of care and attention on every aspect of their studio work, Led Zeppelin really came alive when they got up on stage. Through relentless touring – in the sixteen months between December 1968 and April 1970 they crammed in five tours of the States alone – they were able to create a powerful and loyal fan base that not only wanted to see Led Zep live but also went out and bought their studio albums in droves. After a year or so they sloughed off the need for support acts so that their lengthy two-hour-plus sets could run on without the danger of curfew-careful promoters pulling the plug. Live Led was the message. The band rarely performed on television, a choice emphasised by their decision not to release any singles in the UK. Interviews in the music papers were relatively infrequent: after some bad press in the early days they were wary of the papers. If you wanted to see Page, Plant & co., you had to see them on stage, where their act was all about high-energy, high-decibel power rock that could create an adrenaline high for the audience and performers alike – Melody Maker's Roy Hollingsworth described the mood at a 1971 gig as 'excitement, and something rude, something so alive it smells.' The first market to fall to the onslaught – by design – was America, where manager Peter Grant had landed a monster deal with Atlantic. It took the Brits a little longer, and the relationship between Led Zeppelin and their home fans was not fully consummated until their acclaimed 1970 appearance at the Bath Festival. Thereafter Led Zep's audience never really evolved: the band didn't strain to cross over out of the rock market; they never needed to.

There's only one way a band can
function, and that's on the bloody stage.
Robert Plant

Their live strength was a vital part of their success in the States, a territory their manager Peter Grant decided to concentrate on. Led Zeppelin were the first major UK band to focus their efforts on the US – signing to Atlantic Records, for example – rather than their home market.

Led Zeppelin hit American shores for the first time in late December of 1968 with an awesome fury and a Herculean stamina that even Cream and Hendrix had not prepared anyone for.

Rolling Stone, 1987

Zeppelin started in the States on Boxing Day 1968. Three of the group had never been to America before and didn't know what to expect. My instructions were to go over there and really blast them out. They really did that. Maybe they weren't the greatest thing ever on that first trip, but they got themselves across and the enthusiasm just exploded.

Peter Grant, Led Zeppelin's manager

Before they saw us in America there was a blast of publicity and they heard all about the money being advanced to us by the record company. So the reaction was – 'Ah, a capitalist group'. They realised we weren't when they saw us playing a three hour non-stop show every night.

Jimmy Page,
Melody Maker, 1970

We aren't going to mess around – we're just going to play.
Robert Plant, St Louis, Missouri, 1977

The sheer scale of their shows, their straightforward, hard, bluesy rock, and their position as the most commercially successful act in rock made them an obvious target for punk hostility, as one of the 'dinosaur' supergroups of the mid-Seventies.

Robert Plant came down The Roxy surrounded by millions of bodyguards. I just looked at him, and he's like a real ignorant old northerner, and I felt really sorry for him. Now, how can you respect someone like that?

Johnny Rotten, 1977

Those accusations that were levelled at Zeppelin at the end, during punk, those accusations of remoteness, of playing blind, of having no idea about people or circumstances or reality – there was a lot of substance in what was being said. It hurt at the time, but I'd have to plead guilty.

Robert Plant, *Q* magazine, 1988

Led Zeppelin? I don't need to hear the music – all I have to do is look at one of their album covers and I feel like throwing up.

Paul Simonon, The Clash

I liked the energy of what they were doing, musically, but I didn't pay much attention to what they were saying in the press because I knew that was just a good way of being able to come up with some controversy.

Jimmy Page, 1988

The film, *The Song Remains The Same*, released in 1976, the Year of Punk, was an uneasy marriage of live footage and fantasy features. It missed the mood of the times, and was critically panned.

Far from a monument to Zeppelin's stardom, *The Song Remains The Same* is a tribute to their rapaciousness and inconsideration.
Dave Marsh, *Rolling Stone,* 1976

It's not a great film . . . just a reasonably honest statement of where we were at that particular time.
Jimmy Page

The Zep movie is sort of what would have happened if *Help!* had taken itself seriously as film noir. And been written and produced, directed and edited by junior college students who had just discovered LSD.
Robert Duncan, *Circus*

The most expensive home movie ever made.
Peter Grant, Led Zeppelin's manager

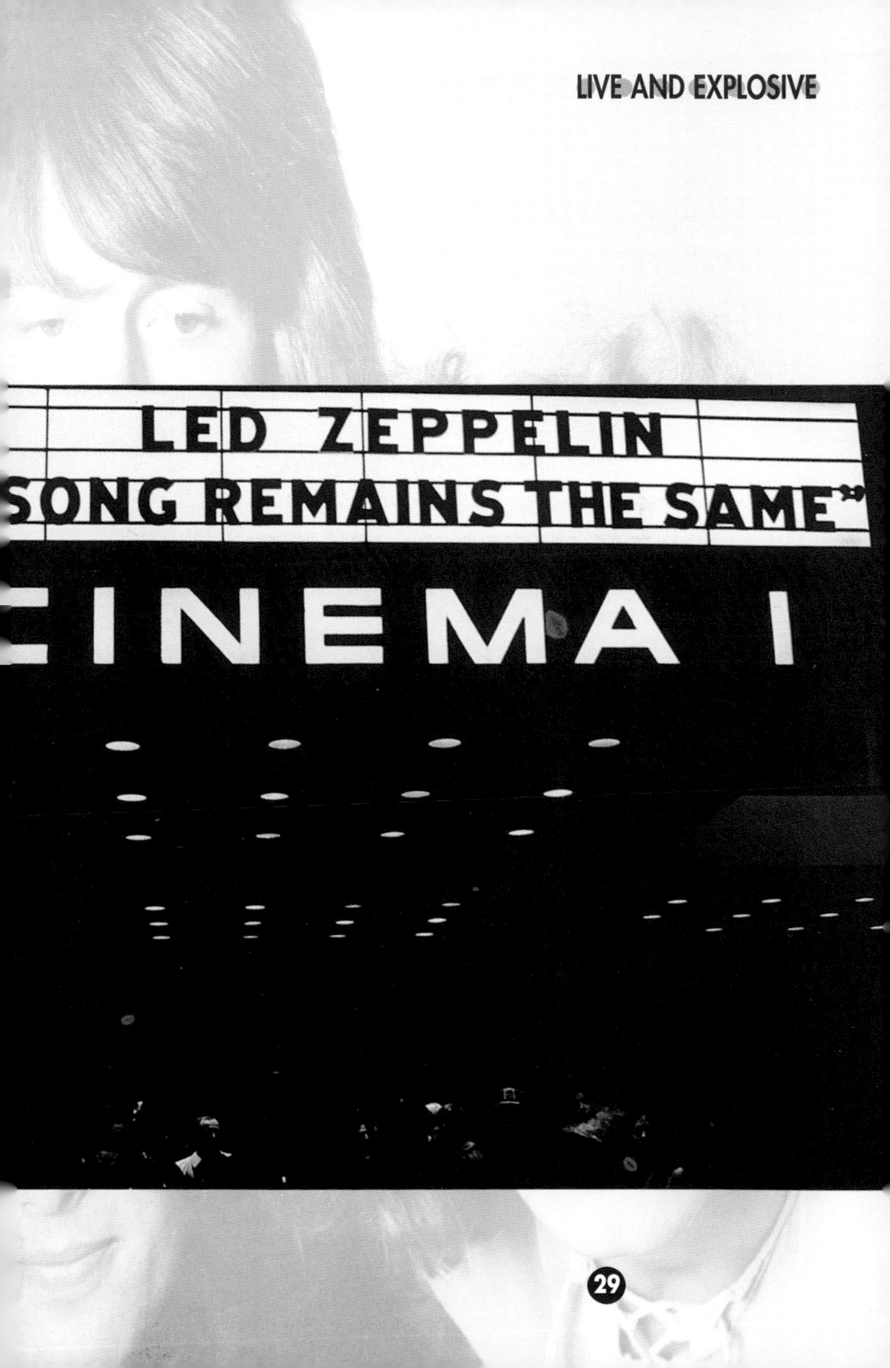
LED ZEPPELIN
SONG REMAINS THE SAME"
CINEMA I

ROCK'N'ROLL ANIMALS

Led Zeppelin, a band whose musical sound was for the most part straightforward and uncomplicated, nonetheless proved a fertile source for some of the most convoluted, apocryphal tales that have grown up around any major act. It was partly their own fault. Given the limited number of interviews they allowed, it was left for the idle gremlins of speculation to fill the column inches instead. The group seemed to want to cultivate an air of mystery – the arcane

symbols that acted as the title for their fourth album were the badges of a secret society where membership was for Led Zep fans only – and Jimmy Page's flirtations with the occult fuelled talk of pacts with the Devil and all kinds of other fanciful nonsense. In addition, from the earliest American tours onwards, rumours of another kind of devilish behaviour, excessive debauchery on tour, began to circulate. Who knows the truth? Here were four famous musicians, including at least one sex god, out on the road, earning substantial amounts of money, letting off plenty of steam. The band always claimed they were no wilder than any other band of the period, that they felt positively tame in comparison with the likes of The Who, that John Paul Jones liked to remain low-key, Bonzo preferred his beer, and Robert Plant wanted to rest his voice between shows . . . . According to them, most of the high jinks were enjoyed by the road crew. But, courtesy of stories about a naked Jimmy Page being delivered on a trolley to a hotel room full of women, or of groupies interfacing with a variety of live seafood, their reputation developed its own momentum, swirling and surging around the reality of their lives. Plant said that in the end he found it fun to linger in the middle and watch people confronting and responding to the reputation. And for a large

percentage of the band's male audience the stories, true or not, served to enhance the impression that these four guys lived out the kind of macho, cock rock fantasies that the sadder fans only wished they could indulge in.

We were in the Midwest and I said to the hotel clerk that it must be tough to have all the rock groups in there throwing furn-iture and TVs out the windows, and he said that they had something worse once . . . and that was the Young Methodists Convention.

Peter Grant

On later American tours, the band would cruise from gig to gig in their customised private jetliner, the 'Starship' – a forty-seat luxury Boeing 720B, which sported a bar, video screens, bedrooms and fireplaces, and suggested a presidential lifestyle which created a benchmark for subsequent bands on tour. It all helped assuage the pain of being on the road.

You must keep going no matter what happens and that's hard when you're getting on a bit. Touring, though, is a real 1,000 miles an hour speed trip – with that power rush you get of actually performing before large crowds every night – and that's why it's worth carrying on.

Robert Plant, *Creem,* 1974

Touring makes you a different person, I think. You always realise it when you come home after a tour. It usually takes weeks to recover after living like an animal for so long.

John Paul Jones

Spinal Tap and The Bad News Thing, they're classic. They really sum up the nightmare aspects of it, everyone can relate to it. Curiously enough there's a bit in Spinal Tap where they can't find the stage and it was very similar to when we were at Madison Square Garden . . . .

Jimmy Page, *Q* magazine, 1988

Semi-official biographies would downplay Zeppelin's on the road activities and the tales of debauchery that have passed into rock legend. In any event, off tour the band went their separate ways.

We never socialised. That's why it lasted so long, I think. We got on the road and everyone was really pleased to see each other. We get back to Heathrow and everyone goes 'Bye!'
John Paul Jones, *Mojo,* 1994

John Paul is the antithesis of a pop star. You never see him. He's like a recluse and only comes out when there's a concert to play or record to make.
Peter Grant, *Daily Mirror,* 1970

35

The ultimate rock'n'roll animal –
in the sense of someone who
understood exactly how the whole
business ticked – was fifth member, the
band's ebullient manager Peter Grant.

I have no musical knowledge, but it's
purely a feeling thing with me. It's not
just liking the sound you hear, it's a
feeling that it's either got the magic or
it hasn't. I can't define it, but it works.
Peter Grant

Grant would say to promoters, Okay,
you want these gigs but we're not
taking what *you* say, we'll tell you what
we want and when you're ready to
discuss it you can call *us*. Peter changed
the rules. He rewrote the book. If we
were the Gods, Grant was The Hammer.
Robert Plant, *Q* magazine, 1988

THE AXEMAN COMETH

● ●

Already an established name when Led Zep began, Jimmy Page's fretmanship alone might have guaranteed him the status of an icon. His position as guitarist in the Yardbirds line-up, from 1966 through to the summer of 1968, had given him access to the exclusive and highly talented heritage of Eric Clapton and Jeff Beck. It also offered him the first chance to build a public profile: within professional music circles, he had been a noted session guitarist for years, credits included work with the Stones, The Who on the 'My Generation' album, maybe even The Kinks on 'You Really Got Me' (although the Davies brothers denied it). He'd also added a helping hand to the Tom Jones 1965 standard 'It's Not Unusual'. Page had developed his skills through self-taught persistence. He'd take his guitar, a steel-stringed acoustic he'd been given in his early teens, to school, where they'd confiscate it during lessons, but return it in time for Jimmy to spend the evenings practising, learning note for note the licks of Bert Jansch, Scotty Moore from Elvis's band, or Ricky Nelson sideman James Burton. Encouraged by his friend Jeff Beck, Page stuck with it, and was able to ride the mid-Sixties R&B boom, establishing himself as a back-room star, and adding his guitar work (usually uncredited) to a vast array of releases. After his stint in the public eye with the Yardbirds, and when that group broke up, he found himself with a clutch of concert obligations to fulfil. It was time to put a new band together: Page, without doubt, was the original creative force behind Led Zeppelin. He remained its musical visionary, producing the albums and crafting the sound. But he was never bigger than the band he created. Led Zep was not simply a vehicle for his guitar talents, although it allowed him ample space to show them off. Page realised that the greatest potential lay in the combined force of all the components.

I just wanted my old partner around for a bit. I wanted to see him swaying around, leaning around so his hair was dangling on the floor. Everyone in the control room was going 'God, look at that man play'. I was sitting there feeling very proud.

Robert Plant, on Jimmy Page guesting on Plant's 1988 solo album 'Now And Zen'

Page was not just a talented guitarist: he was a showman, renowned for his onstage virtuosity, and his party piece – playing the guitar with a violin bow, a trick he'd developed during an idle moment as a session musician. Accordingly, a Melody Maker headline dubbed him 'The Paganini of the Seventies'.

During 'Dazed And Confused' he grabbed a violin bow, and holding the tip-end about two feet away from the strings, coaxed eerie, shivering riffs from his guitar. He leapt into the air and, using the bow like a fencing foil, precisely hit each string at point-blank range and never missed a beat.
Pillow magazine, 1972

It was suggested to me by one of the violinists in the string section. It obviously looks a bit gimmicky because one hasn't seen it done before, and as soon as you pick up a bow and start playing guitar with it . . . . The fact is it's very musical, it sounds like an orchestra at times.
Jimmy Page

In performance, Page's Les Paul Standard was slung low as he prowled the stage. The Les Paul had become the guitar for the blues boom, made popular by Keith Richards and Eric Clapton.

I chose that Les Paul Custom purely because it had three pick-ups and such a good range of sounds – it seemed to be the best all-rounder at the time . . . . Eric must take the credit for establishing the 'Les Paul Sound'.

Jimmy Page, *Zigzag,* 1972

It's showmanship. He curls it all down silent, then barks out like an electric dog with loads of sharp bits of bone in his mouth. He moves well, all the tricks, sneaking about. It's a gorgeous action to watch.

Roy Hollingworth, *Melody Maker,* 1971

Behind the guitar flashiness was an introverted, private man, the creator of Led Zeppelin's sonic panorama. He really cared about the music: when the Led Zeppelin back catalogue was first re-issued lesser quality, second generation tapes were used. Page went back and personally supervised a remastered version from the original masters to ensure the authenticity of his aural landscape.

It's just a chord or a riff that inspires me and then I go on and see how it goes colour-wise. The whole thing just grows like an acorn or something.

Jimmy Page, *Disc,* 1970

When I heard Zeppelin, it was like, OK, now I know why I'm not doing well on my classical piano. Because Jimmy Page was the bridge from acoustic to electric music. He showed me what I could do.

Tori Amos, *Q* magazine, 1995

PURE PERCY

Robert Plant – like The Who's Roger Daltrey – was a front man pure and simple. No instrument, just that voice, but that was plenty. It was a voice that had already caused a stir on the Midlands circuit, when at sixteen Plant had abandoned a chartered accountancy course after two weeks, and set out to try his luck in various local bands, including the Crawling King Snakes, which featured John Bonham on drums. Commercial interest was slow in coming, though, and despite a deal with CBS which produced a couple of forgotten singles, Plant returned to his home base with few obvious prospects. His latest vehicle, at the time he got the call of destiny from Jimmy Page, was an outfit rejoicing in the name of Hobbstweedle (this was the late Sixties). It was Plant's voice which focused Page's mind, as the guitarist was pulling together the ingredients of Led Zeppelin. At the time he was torn between a hard rock sound, and a gentler Incredible String Band approach – the folksy, acoustic sound that would emerge in Led Zeppelin's repertoire later on. In his quest for a new vocalist, Page had looked at a number of candidates: Chris Farlowe, Joe Cocker, and Terry Reid, the vocalist with Peter Jay and the Jaywalkers were all possibles. But when he heard Plant, on Terry Reid's advice, the way forward became clear to him. Ensconced in the limelight of the band, Plant's looks and stage presence provided a focus

for the stage act, but behind the strutting was a reflective side which was exacerbated by the difficulties in his personal life. A car smash in Greece during a 1976 vacation left his wife Maureen in hospital with severe fractures. Plant himself was in plaster and barely able to walk for months afterward. Within twelve months his five-year-old son Karac had died, the victim of a viral infection, while his father was away on another US tour. As Plant later said 'When I lost my boy, I didn't really want to go swinging around – 'Hey hey mama say the way you move' didn't really have a great deal of import any more.'

His voice had an exceptional and distinctive quality. What amazed me more than anything else, especially after the first LP was finished, was that nothing significant had happened to him before.

Jimmy Page, Zigzag, 1973

Plant was the horny rock god that all spotty teenage boys in the Seventies aspired to – in their dreams. Tumbling blonde curls, toe-curlingly tight jeans, a chest he could flaunt without embarrassment: his stage presence was sometimes so extravagantly macho that it was rumoured Jimmy Page considered dropping him during their first US tour.

Good to listen to Plant with his ugly, angry vocals bellowing to his woman that he's gonna leave her right after the next fuck.
Oz review, 1968

If any of my movements appear sexual then they are just accessories to the music at that point in time.
Robert Plant, *Melody Maker, 1977*

Off the road, Plant cultivated a gentle pastoral image. He bought a farm near Kidderminster, as well as a sheep farm in Wales and Bron-Y-Aur, the cottage in Snowdonia where much of 'Led Zeppelin III' had been written. Here he could retire between the rigours of touring to recuperate and recharge.

I think I could sing and shear a few sheep at the same time.
Robert Plant, *NME,* 1974

It gives me room to think, to breathe and live. I wake up in the morning and there are no buses and no traffic. I just revel in these country things. Chickens and goats and me horse. After reading Tolkien I just had to have a place in the country.
Robert Plant

Robert Plant had something of an infatuation with the fantasy figures of English literature, knights and damsels, while Jimmy Page was a fan of occultist Aleister Crowley, buying Crowley's house near Loch Ness, and prompting a media-driven obsession with Zeppelin and the occult that refused to go away.

You see, here I am, the lead singer with Led Zeppelin, and underneath I still enjoy people like Fairport Convention and the Buffalo Springfield. The only heavy band I really dig is the Zeppelin. Apart from that I dig the mellower things.
Robert Plant

He was a huge Celt in those days! I must admit it didn't make much of an impression on Bonzo and I at the time.
John Paul Jones on Robert Plant, *Mojo*, 1994

You can't find anything if you play that song backwards. I know, because I've tried. There's nothing there. We never made a pact with the Devil. The only deal I think we ever made was with some of the girls' High Schools in San Fernando Valley.

Robert Plant on 'Stairway To Heaven', Q magazine, 1988

RHYTHM AND BLUES

Behind the wriggling, writhing Plant and the guitar pyrotechnics of Jimmy Page, the rhythmic heart of the Zep sound was in the hands of John Bonham and John Paul Jones. Bonham was an all-embracing powerhouse with the solidity of sound needed to underpin the two frontmen. Just as Robert Plant had been recommended to Jimmy Page, so Plant had recommended Bonham, who had played with the singer in a couple of bands, to take the drum slot. Bonham, known to one and all as Bonzo (or alternatively as The Beast), was a classic English yeoman, the sort of whole-hearted, ruddy-faced countryman who'd have stood firm at Agincourt or in the squares of Waterloo. His drum sound was equally four-square, and in later years would be sampled far and wide. Jimi Hendrix described him to Robert Plant as having a right foot 'like a pair of castanets'. Jimmy Page simply said he was 'amazingly loud'. Page captured the beef in Bonham's sound, and gave it all the power of cannon shots, by hanging a microphone in the booming hallway of Headley Grange, the Hampshire country house which they first used for recording 'Led Zeppelin III'. Bonham's partner in the rhythm section was the perfect contrast. Quieter, more introspective, Jones had learnt his trade, like Page, on the session circuit. He had brought his multi-instrumental and arranging skills (his father was a pianist and arranger for Forties big bands) to everyone from Herman's Hermits to Lulu and Shirley Bassey. He'd first

met Page on Donovan's 'Hurdy Gurdy Man' album sessions, and they'd worked together again when Jones, in his role as a musical director for Mickie Most, was involved in the recording of the Yardbirds's 'Little Games'. When he heard Page was looking to form a new band, Jones phoned him up. Page leapt at the chance – and throughout Zeppelin's career the bassist added additional layers of musical options, whether on organ, piano or mandolin, or supplying a level of training and experience that helped support Page's own self-taught vision.

Bonham's death – he choked in his sleep after a drinking binge – broke the band's heart. Six weeks after he died, the surviving members of Led Zeppelin issued a brief statement: 'The loss of our dear friend, and the deep sense of harmony felt by ourselves and our manager, have led us to decide that we could not continue as we were.'

There was a period after he died where I just didn't touch a guitar for ages.

Jimmy Page

I did nothing for as long as was respectful to Bonzo, really. Because we *were* best mates. Rather than take the whole Zeppelin thing and try and do it myself, I rejected the whole thing. So I cut my hair off and I never played or listened to a Zeppelin record for two years.

Robert Plant, 1988

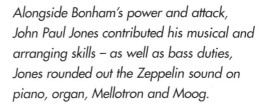

Alongside Bonham's power and attack,
John Paul Jones contributed his musical and
arranging skills – as well as bass duties,
Jones rounded out the Zeppelin sound on
piano, organ, Mellotron and Moog.

Organ, in fact, was always my first
love, but for session playing I found it
much easier to carry a bass guitar to
work than a Hammond organ.
John Paul Jones

He comes along to the studio and
he's always got a new instrument to play.
John Bonham, *Melody Maker,* 1971

He asked me if I could use a bass player in
the new group I was forming. Now John Paul
is unquestionably an incredible arranger and
musician – he didn't need me for a job. John
simply wanted to be part of a group of
musicians who could lay down some good
things. I jumped at the chance of getting him.
Jimmy Page

*The Bonham/Jones combination
clicked straight away at the band's
first rehearsal in September 1968:
they had never met before. Legend
has it that the first track was either
'Train Kept A-Rollin" or Garnett
Mimms's 'As Long As I Have You'.
Jones later recalled that Jimmy
Page counted in whichever song it
was and 'the room just exploded'.*

Bonzo and I connected
immediately, just locked in. Rock
solid and really exciting. Together
we could give Page and Plant the
freedom to go over the top and
add that whole sonic cloud.
John Paul Jones, *Mojo,* 1994

It makes you feel good to hear
Bonham and Jones working
together creating those deep,
surging undercurrents of rhythm
as Page again and again molests
the more vulnerable areas of his
Telecaster.
Felix Dennis, *Oz,* 1968 on the first album

WHOLE LOTTA LED

· ·

Just as Bonham and Jones meshed from day one, so too all four members of Led Zeppelin fitted seamlessly, creating a music that to their legions of fans – predominantly male – was powerful, uplifting, all-consuming. If it wasn't a stairway to heaven, then it was certainly a passage to some other plane. To the band's detractors their music was a lumbering, unimaginative, monotonous, cul-de-sac. Either way Led Zeppelin were the very definition of a rock'n'roll band. They were determined and self-confident, like the airship which had supplied its name (the band also considered calling itself The Whoopee Cushion or The Mad Dogs), Led Zeppelin sailed upwards, powered on by its formula of sledgehammer solid rhythm, soaring, searing guitar, and sexy, scarifying vocals. The individual musicians had diverse musical tastes – Jimmy Page had grown up listening to rock'n'roll with a dose of Bert Jansch's acoustic music, Robert Plant was a blues buff, John Paul Jones added a pop sensibility and a shot of R&B, John Bonham was an early soul fan. Instead of settling for an uneasy amalgam, Led Zeppelin crystallised around rock music in its rawest form, red in tooth and claw, born out of the blues but pumped up into something with its own personality. Although the lawsuit brought by bluesman Willie Dixon might suggest otherwise, the band were not mere blues copyists. Theirs was a larger than life version of the whole thing: nothing fancy, nowhere to hide, unforgettable. It was the power and the energy, pushed to the max, that remained the overriding impression, even when it was balanced by the softer, dreamier side of their output. And

when they tried to move right away from the proven formula, it just didn't work quite so well: on 'Houses Of The Holy' tracks like 'The Crunge' with its cod funk, they sounded uncomfortable. They learnt their lesson – and went back to basics for the next release, 'Physical Graffiti'.

Together on stage, the impact was heightened by the theatrics, including Bonham's flame-circled gong, and his long, long drum solos, a development from the 'Moby Dick' track on 'Led Zeppelin II'.

I really like to yell out when I'm playing. I yell like a bear to give it a boost. I like our act to be like a thunderstorm.

John Bonham

Heard the one about the photographer at Earl's Court whose half-hour allowance fell during Bonham's solitary 40-minute party piece?

Angie Errigo, *NME, 1976*

It's all right when I'm playing.
It only hurts when I stop.

John Bonham, *Melody Maker, 1970*

The power of the Zep sound was the forefather of a later generation of copyists, many of whom caused the members of Led Zeppelin a certain amount of wry amusement (Robert Plant reportedly gave Whitesnake singer David Coverdale the nickname David Coverversion) or sheer frustration.

If I'm responsible for *this*, in any way, then I am really, *really* embarrassed. It's so orderly and preconceived and bleuurghh. Zeppelin, for all their mistakes and wicked ways, were bigger and greater than any of *that* kind of nonsense.

Robert Plant pointing at a Judas Priest poster, Q magazine, 1988

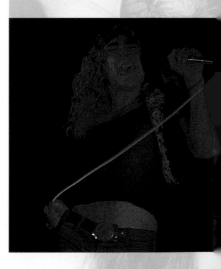

Listening to Zeppelin albums now, you notice everything the macho metallers haven't been able to photo-copy: complexity, subtlety, idiosyncrasy, vision.

Mark Coleman, *Rolling Stone Album Guide*

The name was a suggestion from Keith Moon or John Entwhistle, who said that Page's plan for a new band would go down like a lead balloon – 'lead zeppelin more like'. Peter Grant suggested the spelling Led to make the pronunciation clearer.

Keith Moon came up with Led Zeppelin sometime during our Yardbirds/the New Yardbirds spell and it seemed to fit the bill; we'd been through all kinds of names, like Mad Dogs, for instance, but eventually it came down to the fact that the name was not really as important as whether or not the music was going to be accepted.

Jimmy Page, *Zigzag,* 1973

MUSICAL MOMENTS

Recorded at breakneck speed, 'Led Zeppelin', the debut album, was a snapshot in time of the first few weeks of the band, and the mix of blues and rock they'd tested out on a Scandinavian tour shortly before. With two experienced session musicians, Page and Jones, at the helm, and – at the time – no advance money to fund proceedings, the sessions proceeded with the minimum of wasted effort, capturing all their raw, urgent energy.

Led Zeppelin – the only way to fly.
Ad slogan for the album

The statement of our first few weeks together is our first album. We cut it in fifteen hours and between us wrote six of the nine tracks.
Jimmy Page

Technical, tasteful, turbulent and torrid.
Melody Maker, 1969

The band's first album was a series of controlled explosions. Hoary blues motifs were pumped up to enormous proportions, clubbed senseless by Bonham's colossal wallop, panicked to distraction by Page's crazed air-raid riffs, pummelled by Jones's slum-demolishing bass lines, and strangled by Plant's lascivious shrieks of lust.
Paul Du Noyer, *Q magazine, 1987*

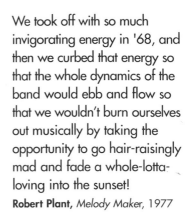

We took off with so much
invigorating energy in '68, and
then we curbed that energy so
that the whole dynamics of the
band would ebb and flow so
that we wouldn't burn ourselves
out musically by taking the
opportunity to go hair-raisingly
mad and fade a whole-lotta-
loving into the sunset!
Robert Plant, *Melody Maker,* 1977

I suppose if we all sat down
and talked about music, John
Paul and Bonzo and I simply
wouldn't agree at all.
Robert Plant, *Melody Maker,* 1970

'Led Zeppelin II' underlined the band's arrival as a major force in rock, going to Number 1 in the UK and US album charts. Written in hotel rooms, rehearsed and recorded on the hoof amid touring obligations, the opening track, 'Whole Lotta Love', was later adopted as **Top Of The Pops**'s theme music throughout the Seventies.

A ragged, nasty projection of male hormonal anguish that's as dangerous if it's feigned as if it's real.
Dave Marsh, *Mojo,* 1994, on 'Whole Lotta Love'

'Whole Lotta Love' is something that I personally need, something I just have to have. We bottle it all up, and when we go onstage we can let it all pour out.
Robert Plant

The famous 'Whole Lotta Love' mix, where everything is going bananas, is a combination of Jimmy and myself just flying around on a small console twiddling every knob known to man.
Engineer **Eddie Kramer**

On the fourth, untitled, album, Page and Led Zeppelin unveiled 'Stairway to Heaven' – eight minutes of music that became the most requested song on American FM radio, was played by every budding music-shop strummer, inspired a complete album of cover versions, and took Rolf Harris back into the charts.

The music came first. I'd written it over a long period; the intro fell into place in Bron-Y-Aur, in the cottage, and other parts came together piece by piece. Robert came out with the lyrics just like that . . . I'd say he produced 40% of the lyrics almost immediately.

Jimmy Page, *Zigzag,* 1973

Everybody can interpret them however they will. It's potential optimism, lyrically. It's saying that if you hold tight, you can make it all right.

Robert Plant on the lyrics

They'd come back from the Welsh mountains with this guitar intro and a verse. I literally first heard it in front of a roaring fire in a country manor house.

John Paul Jones

I thought 'Stairway' crystallized the essence of the band. It had everything there and showed the band at its best. It was a milestone for us.

Jimmy Page

'Physical Graffiti', the band's first album on their own Swan Song label, went gold and platinum on the first day. Their first double album, the lavish die-cut package featured shifting scenes lying behind the windows of a New York brownstone tenement block.

I came up with that title because of the whole thing of graffiti on the album cover and it being a physical statement rather than a written one, because I feel that an awful lot of physical energy is used in producing an album.

Jimmy Page

It's not the kind of music you play before breakfast unless you wake up in a particularly aggressive mood.

NME, 1975

If I'm going to blow my own trumpet about anything I've been connected with, then it would have to be that album.

Robert Plant, *Mojo, 1995*

A work of genius, a superbly performed mixture of styles and influences. They can take as long as they like with the next album: 'Physical Graffiti' will last 18 months or 18 years. And then some.

Melody Maker, 1975

THE MUSIC

★★★★★   **Essential listening**
★★★   **OK**
★   **Frankly, not the best!**

Led Zeppelin – January 1969 ★★★
Good Times Bad Times/Babe I'm Gonna
Leave You/You Shook Me/Dazed
And Confused/Your Time Is Gonna
Come/Black Mountain Side/
Communication Breakdown/I Can't Quit
You Baby/How Many More Times

Jimmy Page triumphs! While long hailed as
one of the British guitar slinging heroes, he
has been a rather mystical figure to British
fans . . . now, with his own group, the legend
comes to life. His band is imaginative and
exciting. Their material does not rely on
obvious blues riffs, although when they do
play them, they avoid the emaciated
feebleness of most so-called British blues bands.
Melody Maker, 1969

Led Zeppelin II – October 1969 ★★★★
Whole Lotta Love/What Is And What Should Never Be/The Lemon Song/Thank
You/Heartbreaker/Livin' Lovin' Maid (She's Just A Woman)/Ramble On/Moby
Dick/Bring It On Home
Hey man, I take it all back! This is one fucking heavyweight of an album! OK – I'll
concede that until you've listened to the album eight hundred times, as I have, it
seems as if it's just one especially heavy song extended over the space of two whole
sides. But, hey! you've go to admit that the Zeppelin have their distinctive and
enchanting formula down stone-cold, man.
John Mendelsohn, *Rolling Stone*, 1969

Led Zeppelin III

– October 1970 ★★★★★
ImmigrantSong/Friends/Celebr
ation Day/Since I've Been
Loving You/Out On The
Tiles/Gallows Pole/Tangerine/
That's The Way/Bron-Y-Aur
Stomp/Hats Off To (Roy) Harper

They have produced a
beautifully creative programme
which spans as many moods as
a wide-screen epic. The best
way to dig 'III' is to put on
head-phones, close eyes and
light a cigarette. From the
opening bars of 'Immigrant
Song' with its thumping,
aggressive 'out of my way' riff
we know they mean business.
Chris Welch,
Melody Maker, 1970

Untitled – November 1971
★★★★★
Black Dog/Rock And Roll/
The Battle Of Evermore/
Stairway To Heaven/Misty
Mountain Hop/Four Sticks/
Going To California/When The
Levee Breaks

The march of the dinosaurs that
broke the ground for their first
epic release has apparently

vanished, taking along with it the splattering electronics of their second effort and the leaden acoustic moves that seemed to weigh down their third.
Lenny Kaye, *Rolling Stone,* 1971

The last album was a very positive move away from what we'd come to expect from the band, but this one gives you the best of both worlds – the excitement of the rock and rolling Zeppelin, and the beauty of the acoustical side they are more and more into.
Billy Walker, *Sounds,* 1971

Houses Of The Holy – March 1973 ★★★
The Song Remains The Same/The Rain Song/Over The Hills And Far Away/The Crunge/Dancing Days/D'Yer Mak'er/No Quarter/The Ocean

Went platinum – 6 times – made it to Number 1 in both the UK and US. It also broke Led Zep's musical mould with the addition of reggae, soul and folk elements to the songs.

Physical Graffiti
– February 1975 ★★★★1/2
Custard Pie/The Rover/In My Time Of Dying/Houses Of The Holy/Trampled Under Foot/Kashmir/In The Light/Bron-Y-Aur/Down By The Seaside/Ten Years Gone/Night Flight/The Wanton Song/Boogie With Stu/Black Country Woman/Sick Again

'Physical Graffiti' is confirmation that the band have lost none of their inspiration and ability, even if it did take them a long time to deliver. It's not the kind of music you play before breakfast unless you wake up in a particularly aggressive mood.
Steve Clarke, NME, 1975

Presence – March 1976 ★★1/2
Achilles Last Stand/For Your Life/Royal Orleans/Nobody's Fault But Mine/Candy Store Rock/Hots On For Nowhere/Tea For One

The Soundtrack From The Song Remains The Same
 – November 1976 ★★
Rock And Roll/Celebration Day/The Song Remains The Same/The Rain Song/Dazed And Confused/No Quarter/Stairway To Heaven/Moby Dick/Whole Lotta Love

Overblown and derivative of Led Zep's own material the album was released at the start of the punk era and represented the sort of bombastic self-indulgence that was so despised by the rebellious youth of the seventies.

In Through The Out Door – August 1979 ★★★
In The Evening/South Bound Saurez/Fool In The Rain/Hot Dog/Carouselambra/All My Love/I'm Gonna Crawl

'In Through The Out Door' became Led Zep's eighth consecutive Number 1 in the UK. Also made it to Number 1 in the US. The record was released in six different sleeves and has sold over 5 million copies worldwide.

Coda – November 1982 ★★1/2
We're Gonna Groove/Poor Tom/I Can't Quit You Baby/Walter's Walk/Ozone Baby/Darlene/Bonzo's Montreux/Wearing And Tearing

Very much an afterthought with some of the flavour and energy but this post Bonzo release contains unreleased songs of interest to purists but lacking the inspirational edge which had made them the world's number one rock-and-roll band.

THE HISTORY

Key Dates

July 1968
The Yardbirds split, leaving guitarist Jimmy Page with the name and a tour of Scandinavia to complete. After Yardbirds bassist Chris Dreja decides not to join Page's new line-up (Dreja pursues a career as photographer instead), Page links up with experienced session man and arranger John Paul Jones, who has picked up on the musicians' grapevine that Page needs help. The line-up is completed by Plant and Bonham, who know each other from the Midlands music circuit.

September 1968
The group begins rehearsals at Jimmy Page's flat in London. Working around a repertoire of blues and R&B numbers, topped up with some Yardbirds tracks, the four musicians click straight away. The line-up fulfils the Scandinavian tour obligations as the New Yardbirds.

October 1968
The group debut as the re-named Led Zeppelin at Surrey University, followed three days later by an appearance as the New Yardbirds again at London's Marquee Club (their last show under that name is the following night at Liverpool University). Their first album, simply called 'Led Zeppelin', is recorded in not much more than thirty hours of work at Olympic Studios in Barnes, London.

November 1968
The band's manager Peter Grant signs them to Atlantic Records, with – at the time – the largest-ever advance paid to a rock band ($200,000, for a five year contract).

December 1968
Led Zeppelin's first tour of the US opens at Denver, Colorado – from the outset they make an impact, marking the start of Zep's huge Stateside success.

January 1969
Their debut album is released first in the US and goes to Number 10 – it will reach Number 6 in the UK following its March release there. Jimmy Page later picks out a series of dates in January at the Fillmore West in San Francisco (supporting Country Joe & The Fish) as the moment when they really broke through in the US.

March 1969
Led Zeppelin's first – and last – UK TV performance is on a show called How It Is.

April 1969

Having won over British audiences during
an 18-date tour, the group head back to the
US for their first headline tour there, opening
at their touchstone venue, the Fillmore West,
and kicking off a five-week sell-out tour,
primarily supported by Julie Driscoll and
Brian Auger & The Trinity. This tour is the
first to spawn rumours of the off-stage, hotel
room shenanigans that will become the
stuff of legend.

June 1969

As hot in the UK as they are in the US,
another string of British dates includes a
performance at the Bath Festival of Blues
and Progressive Music – which provides
the band with their largest UK audience (12,000) to date – and an ecstatic
reception at the first night of the Royal Albert Hall's Pop Proms.

July 1969

Their gruelling assault on the US continues with a series of performances at
America's top jazz festivals – Newport, Baltimore and Philadelphia – and continues
through the summer including dates with The Doors and Jethro Tull.

October 1969

Back in the US again, following a well-deserved break and work on the second
album (mainly written and recorded on the road), Led Zeppelin play at Carnegie
Hall, NYC to open the tour, ending a five-year ban on rock bands at the venue,
imposed after a Stones gig in 1964.

December 1969

'Led Zeppelin II', released in October, reaches the top of the US album charts,
having been kept off the top for two months by the Beatles's 'Abbey Road'.
Advance orders alone had reached 400,000 sales and the album goes on to sell
over six million units in the States.

January 1970
The single 'Whole Lotta Love', taken from 'Led Zeppelin II' and cut down to fit the timing requirements of American radio, reaches Number 4 in the US. The track is their only single to go gold in the US – in the UK they never release any singles. A short UK tour has no support act, allowing Led Zep to spread out their set for over two hours without worrying about curfews at the venues.

February 1970
The second album gets to Number 1 in the UK in the month that the band play in Copenhagen under the name The Nobs. This is due to a threat of legal action, should they use the family name in Denmark, by Eva von Zeppelin, relative of the airship designer. She says 'They may be world famous, but a couple of screaming monkeys are not going to use a privileged family name without permission'.

May 1970
After yet another tour of the States – the band's fifth since late 1969 – Led Zeppelin take a breather. Plant and Page head off to Bron-Y-Aur, a peaceful cottage in the Welsh countryside, where some new songs are written. The band then get together to start work on their third album at Headley Grange, a country house in Hampshire, using a mobile recording studio.

June 1970
A second appearance at the Bath Festival is in front of over 150,000 people, and attracts major British music press attention. Deemed to be Led Zeppelin's real breakthrough in Britain, this is the UK equivalent of their seminal Fillmore West gigs in the US the year before.

September 1970
The band are voted Top Group (both British and International) in Melody Maker's National Pop Poll, finally toppling the Beatles who have been resident in the category for years.

October 1970
Release of 'Led Zeppelin III'. Despite the apparent change to a predominantly acoustic feel, a change which most critics respond to badly, the album is Number 1 in both the UK and US.

March 1971
The band play a series of dates – the 'Return To The Clubs' tour – at those smaller UK clubs and ballrooms where they first played in 1968, after the Yardbirds split. The deal is that the band agree to perform for their original 1968 fee, if the promoters will keep the ticket prices down at 1968 levels. During

a gig in Dublin, the band unveil 'Stairway To Heaven' from their forthcoming album, recorded December 1970-February 1971.

July 1971
A European tour is blighted by rioting in Milan at the Vigorelli Stadium. John Paul Jones later describes the mayhem as 'a war'. A North American tour follows, as well as the band's first dates in Japan.

November 1971
The band put out their untitled fourth album, known variously as 'Led Zeppelin IV', 'Four Symbols', 'The Runes' or 'Zoso' after the mystical images on the sleeve. Number 1 in the UK and Number 2 in the US, where it remains in the album charts for nigh on five years, and sells some 11 million units. The album includes the Zeppelin classic 'Stairway To Heaven' which becomes one of, if not the most played rock track on AOR radio of all time.

February 1972
On the way to a tour of Australasia, a scheduled gig in Singapore is cancelled as the band are not allowed to enter the country. The reason: the length of their hair.

June 1972
Led Zeppelin's eighth tour of the States is yet another sell-out: later in the year, an 18-city British tour sells 120,000 tickets in one day.

March 1973
'Houses Of the Holy' released during a series of European tour dates – the album again reaches Number 1 on both sides of the Atlantic, despite the lack of critical acclaim. The title is reportedly a lyrical description of Led Zeppelin audiences and the venues they fill.

May 1973
Zeppelin's gig at Tampa Stadium, Florida breaks the US box office record previously held by the Beatles for Shea Stadium in 1965. The 33-date tour it forms part of will reportedly earn Led Zeppelin over $4.5 million.

July 1973
The band's three nights at Madison Square Garden are filmed, and the live footage will feature in the movie The Song Remains The Same, although the finished version of the film is not released until 1976. During the same dates, $200,000 of the band's money disappears, and manager Peter Grant is arrested after a scuffle with a photographer. After the tour, the group members work through the Autumn on their individual fantasy sequences for the movie.

May 1974
Swan Song, Zeppelin's own label, is launched. It will release all their own future albums (with distribution by Atlantic), as well as records by Roy Harper, Bad Company, Maggie Bell, the Pretty Things, Dave Edmunds and Detective.

October 1974
Bad Company's first release gives Swan Song a boost by reaching the top of the US album charts (it had been Number 3 in the UK).

January 1975
After a long absence (for Led Zep) from live performance, the band return to the stage with a couple of European dates as preparation for their tenth US tour, another monster outing.

February 1975
The band's first album on Swan Song, 'Physical Graffiti' goes on to continue their record of topping both the UK and US charts.

August 1975
Following five sell-out gigs at Earl's Court, London in May, the band are in tax exile, preparing for a second major US tour that year. However Plant and his wife Maureen are seriously injured in a car smash while holidaying in Greece: Maureen's skull and pelvis are fractured, Plant has fractures of his elbow and ankle. He is out of action for months, and the US tour has to be cancelled. During the enforced break the band concentrate on recording the next album.

March 1976
The 'Presence' album is released – almost inevitably another double Number 1.

October 1976
The premiere of The Song Remains The Same film is held in New York, raising money for the Save The Children Fund: the soundtrack album, released in November, charts at 1 in the UK and 2 in the US.

April 1977
After one false start, when Robert Plant contracts tonsillitis, Led Zeppelin start their first US tour for two years.

July 1977
The American tour, which has been going particularly well, is brought to a sudden end when Robert Plant's 5-year-old son Karac dies from a stomach infection back in the UK; the remaining dates are cancelled, and rumours of an imminent band split abound, fostered by suggestion of a jinx on the band – in September, John Bonham breaks two ribs in a car crash.

November 1978
After an understandably quiet year, Led Zeppelin reconvene to record their ninth album, which cannot be recorded in the UK for tax reasons: the venue chosen is Abba's Polar Studios in Stockholm.

June 1979
Zep return to live performance after a two-year break, with two dates in Copenhagen's Falkonerteatret.

August 1979
The band's first UK date for four years is at the Knebworth Festival, playing to over 300,000 fans over two nights.

September 1979
What turns out to be the band's final studio album, 'In Through The Out Door', again goes to Number 1 in the UK and the US.

June 1980
During a three-week tour of Europe, a concert at Nuremberg in West Germany is cancelled when Bonham collapses – although he recovers and completes the tour.

July 1980
What proves to be Zeppelin's last live concert takes place in West Berlin's Eissporthalle. The final number is 'Whole Lotta Love'.

September 1980
John Bonham found dead at Jimmy Page's home in Windsor, where the band have gathered to rehearse for a North American tour. The coroner's conclusion is that he died from inhaling his own vomit – verdict: accidental death.

December 1980
Led Zeppelin announce that they will not continue following Bonham's death.

November 1982
The album 'Coda' is released: a selection of unreleased tracks selected by Page and containing some overdubs. It reaches Number 4 in the UK and Number 6 in the US.

July 1985
The three surviving Zeps reform for Live Aid at JFK Stadium, Philadelphia, with Phil Collins helping out on drums.

January 1986
The band rehearse for a week with Tony Thompson of Chic on drums but they decide not to re-form.

May 1988
Zeppelin regroup for Atlantic Records's 40th anniversary bash with Bonham's son, Jason, on drums.

May 1989
Peter Grant, Led Zep's manager, announces that the band will never get back together again to tour or record as a group.

October 1994
'Unledded', recorded for MTV's Unplugged series in August, gets the series' highest ratings – Plant and Page appear together, but there is no John Paul Jones. The two subsequently undertake the 'Jimmy Page/Robert Plant World Tour'.

April 1995
Release of 'Encomium: A Tribute to Led Zeppelin', with various artists including Stone Temple Pilots, 4 Non Blondes, Sheryl Crow, Hootie & The Blowfish, and a duet between Plant and Tori Amos.

THE CAST

John Bonham. Born 31 May 1948, Birmingham. Recommended to Jimmy Page by Robert Plant, Bonham is working the Midlands club circuit with group the Band Of Joy. Renowned for his lengthy drum solos and sheer power – he is now reputedly the most sampled drummer in rock history. Bonham is found dead in his bed on 25 September 1980, after a serious 12-hour drinking bout. Within six weeks, the rest of Led Zeppelin decide not to continue. Bonham's son Jason joins the remaining three to re-form Led Zep at Atlantic Records's 40th anniversary celebrations in 1988.

Peter Grant. Born 1944. Moves into rock management via various odd jobs, some TV and film acting and a career as a wrestler with the sobriquet Count Massimo. Works as tour manager for visiting American artists including Gene Vincent, Chuck Berry and the Everly Brothers, then on to managing the Yardbirds, taking over from Simon Napier-Bell. Learns the ropes in the UK and the States, which determines his strategy for Led Zeppelin and will stand Led Zep in good stead. The fiercest and most feared of rock managers – gets things done with no messing. Also manages Bad Company and Maggie Bell in the Seventies; after Zep split retires to his manor house in Sussex. Dies in 1995.

John Paul Jones. Born John Baldwin 3 June 1946, Sidcup, Kent. An experienced session musician, arranger, and multi-instrumentalist – contacts Jimmy Page when he hears latter is looking for new band members. As a session man, Jones, like Page, had worked with a host of artists, including the Stones (on 'Their Satanic Majesties Request'), Dusty Springfield and Donovan. Takes bass and keyboard role within the band, adding textures with Moog and Mellotron, organ and piano. During time with the band writes and produces Madeleine Bell's album 'Comin' Atcha' (and apparently considers quitting to become choirmaster at Winchester Cathedral in 1973). His subsequent career includes production work for acts ranging from Lenny Kravitz to Heart, REM to Diamanda Galas.

Jimmy Page. Born 9 January 1944, Heston, Middlesex. Before forming Led Zeppelin, is a highly rated and much in demand session guitarist in the early Sixties, recording with, amongst many others, Them, Lulu, The Who and Tom Jones (on 'It's Not Unusual'), and some production, including Nico single 'The Last Mile'. Then joins the Yardbirds in June 1966; when that band splits in July 1968 decides to complete a Scandinavian tour with the New Yardbirds. In his quest for replacement band members the four Zeps come together. Following Led Zeppelin's decision to disband after Bonham's death, Page works in various combinations with musicians including Roy Harper, Paul Rodgers (later in a band called The Firm), David Coverdale, as well as own solo work (album 'The Outrider' in 1988),and the occasional Led Zep/Plant and Page reunions.

Robert Plant. Born 20 August 1948, West Bromwich. Invited to join the New Yardbirds after Page and Peter Grant see him performing in Birmingham band called Hobbstweedle, he has previously been in various local R&B groups, including the Crawlin' King Snakes and Band of Joy, with John Bonham. Has also had two solo singles for CBS released in 1966/67. Post-Zep career highlights include solo albums 'Pictures At Eleven' (1982, reaches US Number 5 and UK Number 2), 'The Principle Of Moments' (1983), part-time R&B outfit the Honeydrippers (line-up includes Page, Jeff Beck and Nile Rodgers of Chic), 'Shaken 'n' Stirred' (1985, including Little Feat's Richie Hayward), 'Now And Zen' (1988), 'Manic Nirvana' (1990), 'Fate Of Nations' (1993), before reunion album with Page 'No Quarter' in 1994.

THE BOOKS

Hammer Of The Gods – Stephen Davis (Pan) 1985
Led Zeppelin – Howard Mylett (Granada) 1976
Led Zeppelin: A Celebration – Dave Lewis (Omnibus) 1991
Led Zeppelin: The Definitive Biography – Ritchie Yorke (Virgin) Updated 1993
Led Zeppelin: In Their Own Words – compiled by Paul Kendall
      & Dave Lewis (Omnibus) updated 1985
Led Zeppelin: A Visual Documentary – Paul Kendall (Omnibus) 1982

PICTURE CREDITS

Pages 2-3 Dick Barnatt. **Page 5** Ian Dickson. **Page 8** Chuck Boyd. **Page 23** Ian Dickson. **Pages 24-5** Chuck Boyd. **Page 27** (t) Dave Ellis; (b) Dick Barnett. **Pages 28-9** Richie Aaron. **Pages 30-1** Chuck Boyd. **Page 33** G. Wiltshire. **Pages 34-5** (t) Fin Costello; (b) Ian Dickson. **Page 37** T. Hanley. **Page 39** Richie Aaron. **Pages 40-1** David Redfern. **Page 42** David Redfern. **Page 43** Chuck Boyd. **Pages 44-5** Chuck Boyd. **Pages 46-7** (l) Ian Dickson; (r) Fin Costello. **Page 48** David Redfern. **Page 49** David Redfern. **Page 50 & 51** Ian Dickson. **Pages 52-3** Chuck Boyd. **Page 55** (l) Chuck Boyd; (r) Richie Aarons. **Page 57** David Redfern. **Page 58** Ian Dickson. **Page 59** Chuck Boyd. **Pages 60-1** Ian Dickson. **Page 63** (t) Dick Barnatt; (b) Richie Aaron. **Page 64** (t) Richie Aaron; (b) David Redfern. **Page 66** Fin Costello. **Page 67** Richie Aaron. **Pages 68 & 69** Ian Dickson. **Page 71** (t) David Redfern; (bl) Chuck Boyd; (br) Courtesy of Atlantic Records. **Page 72** (l) Courtesy of Atlantic Records; (r) David Redfern. **Page 73** John Kirk. **Page 74** Chuck Boyd. **Page 75** Chuck Boyd. **Page 76** David Redfern. **Page 77** Courtesy of Atlantic Records. **Page 78** David Redfern. **Page 79** (t) David Redfern; (m) David Redfern; (b) S. Morley. **Page 80** Chuck Boyd. **Page 82** Mick Hutson. **Pages 82-3** Ebet Roberts. **Page 84** Ian Dickson. **Page 85** Chuck Boyd. **Page 86** Chuck Boyd. **Page 87** John Kirk. **Page 90** Dave Ellis. All pictures courtesy of Redferns unless otherwise stated.

Every effort has been made to contact copyright holders. If any ommissions do occur the Publisher would be delighted to give full credit in subsequent reprints and editions.

93